Dedicated to Mother Olga Yaqob.

Thank you for radiating God's
grace and mercy
into the world.

I forgive You

Love We Can Hear, Ask For, and Give

Written by Nicole Lataif

Illustrated by Katy Betz

Pauline
BOOKS & MEDIA
Boston

Library of Congress Cataloging-in-Publication Data

Lataif, Nicole.

  I forgive you : love we can hear, ask for, and give / written by Nicole Lataif ; illustrated by Katy Betz.

       pages cm

  ISBN 978-0-8198-3726-4 -- ISBN 0-8198-3726-1

  1. Forgiveness--Religious aspects--Christianity--Juvenile literature. I. Betz, Katy, illustrator. II. Title.

  BV4647.F55L375 2014

  234'.5--dc23

The Scripture quotations contained herein are from the *New Revised Standard Version Bible: Catholic Edition*, copyright © 1989, 1993, Division of Christian Education of the National Council of the Churches of Christ in the United States of America. Used by permission. All rights reserved.

Book design by Mary Joseph Peterson, FSP

Cover art and illustrations by Katy Betz

"P" and PAULINE are registered trademarks of the Daughters of St. Paul.

Published by Pauline Books & Media, 50 Saint Pauls Avenue, Boston, MA 02130-3491

Printed in the U.S.A.

IFY VSAUSAPEOILL4-110019 3726-1

www.pauline.org

Pauline Books & Media is the publishing house of the Daughters of St. Paul, an international congregation of women religious serving the Church with the communications media.

1 2 3 4 5 6 7 8 9   18 17 16 15 14

For Grown-Ups

"And be kind to one another, tenderhearted, forgiving one another, as God in Christ has forgiven you."

—*Ephesians 4:32*

Forgiving is one of the most difficult things to do, even for the most faithful Christians. How can we teach young children to embrace and share the healing power of forgiveness? *I Forgive You: Love We Can Hear, Ask For, and Give* helps children choose forgiveness by encouraging them to be ready to hear, ask for, and say, "I forgive you."

I Forgive You uses kid-friendly text and images to communicate the most difficult concepts of forgiveness, such as grace, anger, contrition, redemption, and reconciliation. *I Forgive You* brings forgiveness to life, using vivid analogies that offer concrete and clear actions for kids to take.

I Forgive You teaches children that
- we do a lot of things right, but when we don't, God forgives us every time;
- we are called to forgive others as God forgives us;
- forgiveness is a process that may take time and include consequences;
- true friendship has forgiveness;
- holding grudges and feeding anger hurts us most;
- choosing forgiveness brings us peace.

Children will also learn that forgiveness does *not* require that they accept abusive behavior or sustain unhealthy relationships. In these cases, children are encouraged to walk away, tell an adult, pray, and forgive from afar.

This book was created to help you introduce the importance of forgiveness at an early age, open a conversation with the children in your life about forgiveness, and encourage a merciful spirit. The children's forgiveness prayer at the end of the book offers an example of how kids might express their feelings to God.

We all need to ask for and grant forgiveness. God and others forgive us, and in turn, we need to forgive others and, sometimes, ourselves. The most difficult three words to say may be, "I forgive you," yet they are the most important to maintaining good relationships and inner peace. Choosing forgiveness is one of the keys to the love, joy, and peace our faith in Jesus offers us—even for young children!

"Wherever you go, in all that you do, make forgiveness part of you!"

1

Wherever you go,
Whatever you do,
You can hear an "I forgive you."

You do a lot of things right.
But even when you do something wrong,
God loves you.
No matter what you do,
He never says, "I'm through with you!"

God forgives you every time.
He forgives you if you don't share,
If you pull hair,
If you throw a fit,
If you choose to quit.

No matter how big or small,
God forgives it all!

Wherever you go,
Whatever you do,
You can ask for an "I forgive you."

Forgiveness may still mean consequences:
Like lights-out,
Or going without,
Or a timeout.

When you ask for forgiveness, you could say,
I'm sorry I pulled your hair;
I know it made you angry.
I'm sorry I hurt your head.
Would you please forgive me?

But don't just *say* sorry,
Be sorry.

Wherever you go,
Whatever you do,
You can say, "I forgive you."

If your friend breaks your doll,
Or, won't play your games,
Or, loses your ball,
Or, calls you names . . .

You could say,
I'm sad that you won't play my games.
I love playing with you.
There are other things I could do,
But there is only one of you!

Sometimes forgiveness is slow like a snail.
Snails . . .
Take . . .
Forever. . . .
Still, they crawl around freely
    and get where they need to be!

It's okay to take your time.
Forgiveness has no *tick, tock, tick, tock* like a clock.
Forgiveness is not a race.
It is not *vroom, zoom, vroom, zoom* like a car chase.

True friendship has forgiveness.
Not forgiving is scarier than the
meanest monster.
It feels like the slimiest slug.
It smells like the dirtiest dumpster.
It tastes like the biggest bug.

But, be careful.
Forgiveness doesn't mean being like a rug.
Don't let boots walk on you, doing mean things.
Don't let heels dance on you, talking behind your back.
If they do, ask a grown-up for help to walk away.
Forgive from a safe place,
And pray for a change someday.

Wherever you go,
Whatever you do,
Make forgiveness part of you.

Everyone needs to forgive, even the
coolest kid who ever lived.
He may play violin and get all As,
Always come in first place,
And one day even fly to space.
But if he won't forgive—what a waste!

Not forgiving is like having an elephant in your heart.
He grows and grows.
He gets heavier and heavier until . . .
CRACK!
He breaks your heart.

When you feed anger,
    it's like having a lion in your throat.
Lions roar.
Roaring is scary.
Speak calmly instead.
Roaring hurts others, but it hurts you more.
When you're mad, take a break.
Talk it through with someone who loves you.

Forgive others as God does.
You are God's face when you turn your cheek.
You are God's mouth when your words are true.
You are God's arms when you hug hello.
You are God's voice when you say, "I forgive you."

You can only forgive with God's help.
Tell God you are angry.
Tell him you are mad.
Tell him what went wrong,
And what makes you sad.

God knows when you're hurt,
And when you hurt others, too.
Forgiveness brings peace
   to both of you.

Forgiveness soothes like a song.
It mends like a thread.
It heals like a kiss.
It's warm like your bed.

Wherever you go,
Whatever you do,
You can hear . . .
You can ask for . . .
You can say . . .
"I forgive you."
Then, forgiveness will be
part of you.

Children's Prayer

Lord, you are full of mercy and love.
Thank you for forgiving all my sins.
Help me to know how much you love me, even
when I do something hurtful or wrong.

When I hurt someone else, please help me to be
truly sorry.
When I am angry, give me patience.
When I am upset, help me not to take it out on
others.
Give me the courage to ask for forgiveness.
Help me to accept any consequences for things
I've done wrong.

And when I am hurt, help me to heal.
When I am sad, give me hope.
If someone bullies me, make me brave enough to
tell someone who loves me.
Help me to forgive others, even if it takes time.
Remind me to pray for those who have harmed me.
Lord, fill my heart with your mercy.
Make forgiveness part of me, so that I may love
others the way you do.

Amen.

Nicole Lataif

Award-winning author Nicole Lataif wrote her first poem at the age of six in an effort to charm her way out of being sent to her room. It didn't work. She finally got out and has been writing ever since.

After receiving a bachelor's degree in rhetorical studies from Florida Atlantic University, Nicole went on to publish her first children's book, *Forever You: A Book About Your Soul and Body,* winner of the 2013 Christopher Award and a 2013 Catholic Press Association award. *Forever You* is now also available in Spanish as *Siempre Tú.*

Nicole lives in Boston, Massachusetts, where she substitute teaches and leads a writer's group.

She is available for speaking engagements at schools, churches, and community centers across North America. Contact Nicole on her website, www.NicoleLataif.com, where you'll also find resources for teaching Christian virtues to children.

Katy Betz

Katy Betz illustrates in both traditional and digital media. She works in the fields of children's literature as well as gallery and editorial illustration. She is also a professor of illustration at Ringling College of Art & Design in Sarasota, Florida.

Katy's personal artwork focuses on visual narratives inspired by Holy Scripture, history, philosophy, fantasy, and nature. She enjoys imagining stories, worlds, and characters to express ideas that will make an emotional and intellectual connection with her audience. Katy's artistic philosophy is to bring something new, something beautiful, and something filled with light into the world. You can see more of her work at www.katybetz.com.

Who are the Daughters of St. Paul?

We are Catholic sisters. Our mission is to be like Saint Paul and tell everyone about Jesus! There are so many ways for people to communicate with each other. We want to use all of them so everyone will know how much God loves us. We do this by printing books (you're holding one!), making radio shows, singing, helping people at our bookstores, using the Internet, and in many other ways.

Visit our Web site at www.pauline.org

Pauline
BOOKS & MEDIA

The Daughters of St. Paul operate book and media centers at the following addresses. Visit, call, or write the one nearest you today, or find us at www.pauline.org.

CALIFORNIA
3908 Sepulveda Blvd, Culver City, CA 90230 — 310-397-8676
935 Brewster Avenue, Redwood City, CA 94063 — 650-369-4230
5945 Balboa Avenue, San Diego, CA 92111 — 858-565-9181

FLORIDA
145 SW 107th Avenue, Miami, FL 33174 — 305-559-6715

HAWAII
1143 Bishop Street, Honolulu, HI 96813 — 808-521-2731

ILLINOIS
172 North Michigan Avenue, Chicago, IL 60601 — 312-346-4228

LOUISIANA
4403 Veterans Memorial Blvd, Metairie, LA 70006 — 504-887-7631

MASSACHUSETTS
885 Providence Hwy, Dedham, MA 02026 — 781-326-5385

MISSOURI
9804 Watson Road, St. Louis, MO 63126 — 314-965-3512

NEW YORK
64 West 38th Street, New York, NY 10018 — 212-754-1110

SOUTH CAROLINA
243 King Street, Charleston, SC 29401 — 843-577-0175

VIRGINIA
1025 King Street, Alexandria, VA 22314 — 703-549-3806

CANADA
3022 Dufferin Street, Toronto, ON M6B 3T5 — 416-781-9131